BIG AND SMALL ANIMALS

BIRDS

Children's Press®
An imprint of Scholastic Inc.

BY BRENNA MALONEY

A special thank-you to the team at the Cincinnati Zoo & Botanical Garden for their expert consultation.

Library of Congress Cataloging-in-Publication Data
Names: Maloney, Brenna, author.
Title: Birds / by Brenna Maloney.
Description: First edition. | New York, NY: Children's Press, an imprint of Scholastic Inc., 2023. | Series: Big and small animals | Includes index. | Audience: Ages 5–7. | Audience: Grades K–1. | Summary: "Continuation of the Wild World series comparing big and small animal sizes"— Provided by publisher.
Identifiers: LCCN 2022026380 (print) | LCCN 2022026381 (ebook) | ISBN 9781338853506 (library binding) | ISBN 9781338853513 (paperback) | ISBN 9781338853520 (ebk)
Subjects: LCSH: Birds—Miscellanea—Juvenile literature. | CYAC: Birds. | Size. | BISAC: JUVENILE NONFICTION / Animals / Birds | JUVENILE NONFICTION / Concepts / Opposites
Classification: LCC QL676.2 .M3442 2023 (print) | LCC QL676.2 (ebook) | DDC 598—dc23/eng/20220606
LC record available at https://lccn.loc.gov/2022026380
LC ebook record available at https://lccn.loc.gov/2022026381

Copyright © 2023 by Scholastic Inc.

All rights reserved. Published by Children's Press, an imprint of Scholastic Inc., *Publishers since 1920*. SCHOLASTIC, CHILDREN'S PRESS, and associated logos are trademarks and/or registered trademarks of Scholastic Inc.

The publisher does not have any control over and does not assume any responsibility for author or third-party websites or their content.

No part of this publication may be reproduced, stored in a retrieval system, or transmitted in any form or by any means, electronic, mechanical, photocopying, recording, or otherwise, without written permission of the publisher. For information regarding permission, write to Scholastic Inc., Attention: Permissions Department, 557 Broadway, New York, NY 10012.

10 9 8 7 6 5 4 3 2 1   23 24 25 26 27

Printed in China   62
First edition, 2023

Book design by Kay Petronio

Photos ©: 6: Joan Egert/Dreamstime; 8–9: Kevin Schafer/Alamy Images; 10–11: Rick & Nora Bowers/Alamy Images; 11 inset: mura/Getty Images; 16 inset: RUNSTUDIO/Getty Images; 20–21: Chris and Monique Fallows/Minden Pictures; 24–25: blickwinkel/Alamy Images.
All other photos © Shutterstock.

BEE HUMMINGBIRD

COMMON OSTRICH

CONTENTS

Bird Basics 4
#10 Smallest Bird:
   Bee Hummingbird 6
Bee Hummingbird Close-Up 8
#9: Elf Owl 10
#8: Victoria Crowned Pigeon 12
#7: Scarlet Macaw 14
#6: Emperor Penguin 16
#5: Eurasian Black Vulture 18
#4: Wandering Albatross 20
#3: Mute Swan 22
#2: Southern Cassowary 24
#1 Biggest Bird: Common
   Ostrich 26
Common Ostrich Close-Up 28
Birds Big and Small 30
Glossary 31
Index 32

BIRD BASICS

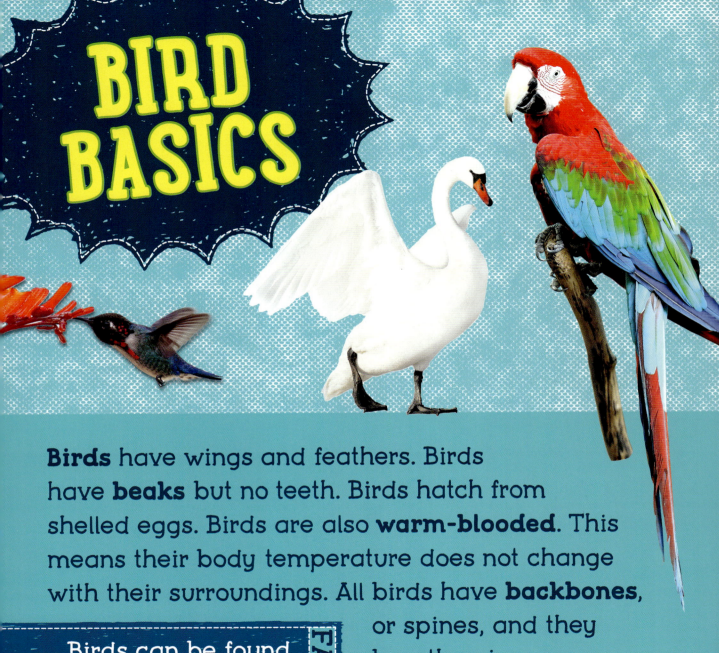

Birds have wings and feathers. Birds have **beaks** but no teeth. Birds hatch from shelled eggs. Birds are also **warm-blooded**. This means their body temperature does not change with their surroundings. All birds have **backbones**, or spines, and they breathe air.

FACT Birds can be found on every continent.

Measuring Up

This book is all about size. Which birds are the smallest? Which are the biggest? Why does being big or small matter? An animal's size can determine where and how it lives. Some birds build big nests. Some nest in tiny spaces. Some birds eat a lot. Other birds eat a little. Some birds are too big to fly. Some are so tiny, they are mistaken for insects. You can learn a lot about birds just by their size.

Get ready to discover the different sizes of 10 amazing birds and why it matters, from the smallest to the biggest!

#10 Smallest Bird: BEE HUMMINGBIRD

Bee hummingbirds are the world's smallest birds. They measure only 2.2 inches (6 cm) in length. These birds are so small, they can be mistaken for bees. When they fly, their beating wings even sound like buzzing bees.

Bee hummingbirds eat insects and sip **nectar**, the sugary liquid found in flowers. As they poke their heads into flower petals to reach nectar, **pollen** sticks to their heads and beaks. That pollen gets moved when birds go to the next flower.

These fast fliers burn a lot of energy flapping their wings 80 times per second. So, they need to refuel every few minutes. In a single day, they might visit 1,500 flowers and eat up to half their weight in nectar.

SAME SIZE AS . . .

The world's smallest bird is as tall as a golf tee.

FACT Bee hummingbirds are found only in Cuba.

BEE HUMMINGBIRD CLOSE-UP

The bee hummingbird is not just the world's smallest bird. It's also the bird with the smallest eggs. Their eggs are the size of coffee beans.

FLIGHT READY
These birds can fly for up to 20 hours without a break and can reach speeds of up to 30 miles per hour (48 kph).

WINGS
A figure-eight movement of the wings allows the bird to **hover** over flowers to eat. These wings can help the bird to fly upward, downward, backward, and even upside down.

WEIGHT
The average weight of a bee hummingbird is 0.06 ounces (2 g).

EYES
Their eyes can pick up colors that humans cannot see.

BEAK
A slender, pointed beak is built for poking deep into flowers.

TONGUE
A long, thin tongue laps up flower nectar.

HEART
A racing heart beats 1,260 times a minute. By comparison, a human's resting heartbeat is usually between 60 and 100 beats per minute.

FEATHERS
Bee hummingbirds have fewer feathers than any other bird.

FACT Bee hummingbirds build the world's smallest bird nests, made from bits of cobweb, tree bark, and plants.

#9 ELF OWL

Elf owls are the world's smallest owls. They stand less than 6 inches (15 cm) tall. They weigh less than 1-1/2 ounces (43 g)—a bit less than a golf ball. These tiny birds are **carnivores.** They have a big appetite for moths, beetles, and crickets. They also gobble up scorpions, spiders, and katydids. Elf owls hunt at night and catch their **prey** in flight, on the ground, or within the trees. The sound of their wingbeat is muffled by the soft feathers on the edges of their wings.

FACT: These owls can be found in the United States and Mexico.

SAME SIZE AS...

An elf owl is no larger than a juice box.

These pigeons are native to the island of New Guinea.
FACT

SAME SIZE AS...

A Victoria crowned pigeon is as tall as a baseball bat.

#8
VICTORIA CROWNED PIGEON

The largest pigeons on Earth are Victoria crowned pigeons. They can grow to be 2.5 feet (76 cm) long and can weigh nearly 8 pounds (4 kg). These birds can fly, but they spend most of their time on the ground in small **flocks**. Together, they work as a team to search the rain forest floor for insects, fruit, and seeds to eat. These pigeons make different sounds for different reasons. They make a deep, human-like *ummm* sound when they are looking for each other.

#7 SCARLET MACAW

Macaws are the largest parrots in the world. From beak to tail, a scarlet macaw can be as long as 2.8 feet (85 cm). These **herbivores** eat seeds, berries, fruit, and especially nuts. Nuts are easily cracked open with their tough beaks. The scarlet macaw can eat fruit that is poisonous to other animals. It eats large amounts of clay, which absorbs the poison.

FACT

All macaws are left-footed. They use their left foot to handle food while they support themselves with their right foot.

SAME SIZE AS . . .

A scarlet macaw is almost as long as a yard stick.

SAME SIZE AS...

An emperor penguin is about as tall as a six-year-old child.

#6
EMPEROR PENGUIN

Emperor penguins are the largest of all penguins. These flightless birds can grow to be 3.8 feet (116 cm) tall. They weigh an average of 88 pounds (40 kg), but their weight changes throughout the year. Before winter, they can eat 6 pounds (3 kg) or more of fish, krill, and squid a day. During winter, males will not eat for four months. While the females go to sea to find food, the males stay behind to **incubate** their eggs.

FACT These penguins are found only in Antarctica.

#5 EURASIAN BLACK VULTURE

The Eurasian black vulture is the largest vulture and the largest bird of prey. These birds can grow up to 3.9 feet (119 cm) tall and can weigh up to 28 pounds (13 kg). Black vultures are **scavengers**. That means they eat the remains of dead animals. These vultures play an important role in nature by eating dead animals before they rot and cause disease. This type of bird is built for the job. Their heads are covered with short feathers so they can eat without getting messy. Their strong, hooked beaks help them tear food apart.

These vultures can live more than 25 years in the wild.
FACT

SAME SIZE AS...
Eurasian black vultures can stand as tall as a standard fence.

SAME SIZE AS...

A wandering albatross is a little taller than a hockey net.

#4 WANDERING ALBATROSS

The wandering albatross is the world's largest seabird. They are an average of 4.4 feet (134 cm) tall and have the largest wingspan of any bird—up to 11 feet (3 m). Despite their enormous wings, these birds rarely flap when they fly. Instead, they use the wind to gain height. Then they glide long distances. Wandering albatross spend all their time at sea, landing only to feed. They can sleep while flying or bobbing in the water.

FACT: These albatross can live more than 60 years.

#3 MUTE SWAN

Mute swans are big birds. They can measure 5.6 feet (171 cm) long. They are also one of the heaviest flying birds. Males can weigh up to 32 pounds (15 kg). Mute swans are **omnivores**. They eat **aquatic** plants, insects, fish, and frogs, and they have enormous appetites! They can eat up to 8 pounds (4 kg) of plants a day. They feed in deeper waters than most water birds, but they don't dive. Instead, they plunge their heads and long necks into the water to look for food.

These swans are less vocal than other swans.
FACT

SAME SIZE AS...

A mute swan is as tall as 4-1/2 bowling pins stacked on top of each other.

SAME SIZE AS...

A southern cassowary is as tall as a refrigerator.

#2 SOUTHERN CASSOWARY

Southern cassowaries are the second-heaviest birds in the world. These flightless birds can reach up to 6 feet (183 cm) tall. They can weigh almost 160 pounds (73 kg). Despite their size, cassowaries are **frugivores**. That means they are animals that mainly eat fruit—as much as 11 pounds (5 kg) a day. The seeds of the fruit they eat pass through their systems when they go to the bathroom. Some of these seeds then take root and grow.

FACT

A razor-sharp claw on the middle toe of each foot helps protect them from **predators**.

#1 Biggest Bird: COMMON OSTRICH

Common ostriches are the largest and the heaviest birds on the planet. They can be more than 9 feet (274 cm) tall and weigh as much as 320 pounds (145 kg).

SAME SIZE AS . . .

A common ostrich can be a little shorter than a standard basketball hoop.

These birds spend most of the day grazing for food. Ostriches eat grasses, shrubbery, berries, and seeds. They also eat insects and small reptiles. Ostriches eat something else, too—rocks! Swallowing small stones helps grind up their food. Ostriches do not need to drink water for short periods of time. They get the water they need from the plants they eat. However, they will take a sip and a dip in any water hole they find.

FACT Ostriches can live for as long as 70 years.

BEAK
The flat and broad beak has a rounded tip.

EYES
More than 2 inches (5 cm) across, an ostrich's eyes are the largest of any land animal. They also have long eyelashes.

THROAT
As an ostrich eats, food is collected at the top of the throat until there is a large enough lump to swallow.

NECK
The long neck keeps the ostrich's head high aboveground so it can spot predators more easily.

STOMACH
An ostrich has three stomachs to help it digest its food.

FACT: Ostrich chicks can run at speeds approaching 35 miles per hour (56 kph) at just a month old!

COMMON OSTRICH CLOSE-UP

The common ostrich is not just the world's biggest bird. It is also the world's fastest two-legged animal. When chased by a predator, the ostrich can run up to 43 miles per hour (70 kph).

WINGS
A common ostrich can't fly. Why does it need wings? It holds its wings out to help it balance when it runs.

FEATHERS
Their feathers don't have the tiny hooks that lock the feathers of flying birds together. Instead, these feathers are soft and fluffy, keep the bird warm, and are not waterproof.

TOES
Ostriches are the only birds that have two toes. All other birds have three or more.

BIRDS BIG AND SMALL

Birds come in all shapes and sizes. Now you know why being a big or small bird matters. There are more than 10,000 **species** of birds in the world—too many to cover in this book! Make it your mission to learn even more about these amazing animals, both big and small.

GLOSSARY

aquatic (uh-KWAH-tik) living or growing in water

backbone (BAK-bohn) a set of connected bones that runs down the middle of the back; also called the spine

beak (beek) the horny, pointed jaw of a bird

bird (burd) a warm-blooded animal with two legs, wings, feathers, and a beak

carnivore (KAHR-nuh-vor) an animal that eats other animals for food

flock (flahk) a group of animals of one kind that live, travel, or feed together, as in a *flock* of birds

frugivore (FROO-juh-vor) an animal that feeds on fruit

herbivore (HUR-buh-vor) an animal that eats plants

hover (HUHV-ur) to remain in one place in the air

incubate (ING-kyuh-bate) to keep eggs warm before they hatch

nectar (NEK-tur) a sweet liquid from flowers that lures pollinators

omnivore (AHM-nuh-vor) an animal that eats both plants and animals

pollen (PAH-luhn) a fine powder produced by certain plants that helps the plants make seeds

predator (PRED-uh-tur) an animal that lives by hunting other animals for food

prey (pray) an animal that is hunted by another animal for food

scavenger (SKAV-uhn-jur) an animal that does not capture its own prey; instead it eats dead animals left by other predators

species (SPEE-sheez) a group of similar organisms that are able to reproduce

warm-blooded (WORM bluhd-id) having a body temperature that does not change, even if the temperature of the surroundings is very hot or very cold

INDEX

Page numbers in **bold** indicate images.

B
bee hummingbird, **4**, **6**, **7**, **8–9**, 30
  diet and eating, 7
  eggs, 8
  flight, 7, 8
  habitat, 7, 9
birds
  common traits of, 4
  flightless. *See* common ostrich; southern cassowary
  number of, 30

C
common ostrich, **26**, **27**, **28–29**, 30
  diet and eating, 27
  lifespan, 27
  speed, 28, 29

E
elf owl, **11**, 30
  diet and eating, 10
  habitat, 10
emperor penguin, **5**, **16**, **17**
  diet and eating, 17
  habitat, 17
Eurasian black vulture, **18–19**
  diet and eating, 18
  lifespan, 19

F
flightless birds. *See* common ostrich; southern cassowary

M
mute swan, **4**, **23**, 30
  diet and eating, 22

P
parrot. *See* scarlet macaw

S
scarlet macaw, **4**, **14–15**
  diet and eating, 14
southern cassowary, **24**
  defense mechanisms, 25
  diet and eating, 25

V
Victoria crowned pigeon, **5**, **12–13**, 30
  diet and eating, 13
  habitat, 12
  sounds, 13

W
wandering albatross, **5**, **20–21**
  flight, 21
  lifespan, 21

ABOUT THE AUTHOR

Brenna Maloney is the author of more than a dozen books. She lives and works in Washington, DC, with her husband and two sons. She wishes she had more pages to tell you about birds. She also wishes she had the smarts of a raven, the stealth of a tawny frogmouth, and the style of a Nicobar pigeon. (Look them up!)